DEADLY
CREATURES

First published in Great Britain by
CAXTON EDITIONS
an imprint of
The Caxton Book Company,
16 Connaught Street,
Marble Arch, London, W2 2AF.

ISBN 1 84067 059 2

A copy of the CIP data for this book is available from the British Library upon request.

With grateful thanks to Morse Modaberi who designed this book.

Created and produced for Caxton Editions by
FLAME TREE PUBLISHING,
a part of The Foundry Creative Media Company Ltd,
Crabtree Hall, Crabtree Lane,
Fulham, London, SW6 6TY.

Printed in Singapore by Star Standard Industries Pte. Ltd.

HEADstart

DEADLY CREATURES

The world's most dangerous animals, in glorious colour

CAMILLA DE LA BÉDOYÈRE

CAXTON EDITIONS

✦ Contents ✦

Introduction

One hundred and forty years ago a scientist, Charles Darwin, suggested that all creatures compete with each other for scarce resources like food, mates or living space. He said that the successful ones would live longer than the weaker ones and be able to breed more offspring (or young).

Deadly creatures have to kill to survive. The African hippopotamus, for example, is responsible for more human deaths when defending its territory than the fearsome crocodile. Its powerful jaws and huge teeth can inflict terrible wounds on an enemy.

Speed, strength, skill and razor-sharp teeth and claws are the weapons of big cats like lions and cheetahs. Killing mainly for food, these beautiful animals have survived for millions of years, although they are now themselves threatened by hunters of the human kind.

Snakes, spiders and scorpions are among the most dangerous of all creatures, often relying on poison (venom) to paralyse and kill. The venom, injected through a sting or hollow teeth, reaches a victim's brain within minutes. One sting from the North African scorpion can cause instant death.

Some of the scariest creatures are those we cannot see. Animals too small to be seen, called micro-organisms, can cause disease and death in animals, plants and humans.

All these creatures have something in common. They have evolved, or developed, over a long time to play a special part in the animal kingdom. Every part is needed to maintain a balance – we call this the earth's ecology. It is our responsibility to conserve this beautiful but fragile balance.

Weapons

Deadly creatures have weapons; often these are ordinary parts of an animal's body which have developed to do a special job.

Antlers and horns, for example, are made of bone and a substance called keratin (which we humans have in our nails and hair). Narwhal, elephant and walrus tusks are all over-grown teeth. Often it is only the males who have these weapons and they are used to fight other males for living spaces (territories) or females – sometimes to

the death. A narwhal's tusk can grow up to 3 metres in length.

Snake fangs are hollow teeth that allow venom to pass through to a victim's flesh: venom is saliva (spit) with added poisons that can paralyse or kill.

The teeth of meat-eaters are sharp and pointed. This makes it easier to grab prey and tear skin. Simply by roaring and showing their teeth lions can frighten their rivals away.

Claws are strong, sharp nails which are powerful enough to grip tightly. A bear's claws can catch and hold a wriggling salmon until his teeth can finish it off. Birds of prey have claws called talons.

Even skin can be a weapon. Some animals produce poisons on their skins that protect them from being eaten. The Choco Indians of South America kill monkeys using poison wiped from the back of arrow-poison frogs, and the skin of a puffer fish is deadly if eaten by a human.

Just one insect bite or sting may be dangerous and when thousands of them swarm together they can be deadly.

Warning Signs

Most animals would prefer to avoid a fight. It saves energy and it stops any chance of them getting hurt. So, unless they are hunting, deadly creatures show warning signs to other animals to prove that they are dangerous and telling them not to get too close.

An animal's size, strength and good health can be enough to make enemies stay away. Large antlers, tusks and horns show a beast is fit and ready to fight. Roaring, growling, stamping and pacing across one's territory are other ways of telling rivals to go or they will get hurt. Chimpanzees, for example, stand tall and beat their chests while grunting loudly.

Colour is one of nature's best warning signs. Bright colours like red, yellow and orange in bold patterns and stripes spell danger. Wasps, coral snakes and arrow-poison frogs are all brightly coloured and dangerous.

Skunks avoid a fight by making an awful smell; they have bold black and white stripes to warn predators of the terrible stink they will create if attacked. If the predator does not take the hint the skunk will point its bottom at it and squirt a foul-smelling liquid.

The Australian blue-ringed octopus is covered with pale blue circles. When the beast is scared the circles turn a deeper peacock blue and the body goes dark – a warning from one of the world's deadliest killers.

Rattlesnake tails contain rings of hardened skin at the tip. These make a well-known rattling noise when shaken – telling any creature nearby that the killer is poised for action.

Elephants, Rhinos and Hippos

A huge African elephant stands before you, flapping enormous ears, stamping the ground, snorting and trumpeting. It is a terrifying sight and you know it is time to escape. Elephants, rhinoceroses and hippopotamuses are all plant-eaters and do not need to kill to eat but their large tusks or horns are deadly weapons which they use to protect themselves and their families.

Elephants live in groups and will attack lions or hyenas who get too close. Sometimes male elephants leave the group and roam on their own. These are called 'rogue males' and they can be very fierce.

The horn of the white rhino can grow up to 1.5 metres long. The rhino sharpens its horn by rubbing it against trees and rocks. Sadly, the rhino is hunted for its horn and there are few rhinos left in the wild. Unless these animals are protected they will soon become extinct.

Elephants and rhinos live in the grasslands of Africa and Asia, and spend most of the day grazing grass and eating leaves. Hippopotamuses live only in Africa and in the daytime can be found in rivers and lakes. At night they come on to land to eat the grass by the water's edge.

Hippos can stay under water for up to five minutes. A boat passing over a hippo is in real danger; a scared hippo may capsize the boat and attack the people inside. Male hippos are fierce fighters, using their strong jaws and tusks to wrestle with each other.

Tigers and Lions

Deep in the lush jungles of India the true king of hunters lives. With ears pricked and eyes peering through the vegetation, the tiger prowls at night. The strongest of all big cats, he stalks pigs and antelope, using his ripping claws, crushing jaws and piercing teeth to kill them.

A tiger's stripes camouflage him in the dense jungle. His sharp eyes and large ears help him to hunt in the dim evening light. Tigers can swim and they have been known to pull people out of boats.

Although greatly feared, tigers rarely kill humans unless they are sick or scared. Once a tiger has killed a human it is known as a 'man-eater'.

Tigers live and hunt alone but lions live in family groups called prides. Seeking out grazing herds, like wildebeest, the lionesses find the weakest animal. Slowly, swiftly, quietly, they creep up behind their chosen prey. The lionesses spread out so that whichever way the wildebeest run there will be a lioness ready to chase it.

With a fast run, and by pouncing on to the terrified animal, the lioness brings it down with a bite on the back of its neck. The rest of the pride can now join in the family feast.

Male lions look fierce with their large manes but they do not often hunt. Instead, they use their fighting skills to keep other males away from their territory and their females. Males fight ferociously to get new mates and some even die from their injuries.

Wolves

Wolves and wild dogs are excellent hunters and can be found in many parts of the world. Like tame dogs they have a keen sense of smell, are good runners and tend to be social animals, preferring to live in groups or packs, rather than by themselves.

For a long time people have been scared of wolves and have told stories, such as *Little Red Riding Hood* and *The Three Little Pigs*, to teach children to stay away from them. But really these creatures are scared of humans and only come close if they are very hungry.

Most types of wolf and wild dog live and hunt in packs as this is a successful way to catch prey. A wolf pack has two leaders; the alpha male and female. They are the only wolves in the pack to have cubs. The alpha pair lead the hunt, prowling through the woods in search of a victim – usually a deer or wild pig.

Once a deer is spotted the wolves spread out. Travelling upwind so the deer cannot smell them, the pack surrounds it. When the deer begins to run the wolves follow. The younger, fitter wolves move to the front of the group, keeping a steady pace. As the prey eventually slows down the wolf pack closes in for the kill. While one wolf jumps on the deer's back another will run to its front and seize its nose, pulling it to the ground. The animal is killed and the wolves can share the meal.

Sharks and Whales

Sharks are the world's largest fish and are so well suited to their environment that they have scarcely changed in 200 million years. Although feared as the deadliest of the sea's creatures, most sharks are not dangerous at all.

The most famous of the deadly sharks is the Great White shark which likes to swim close to the shore, hunting for seals, sea-lions and dolphins. Meat-eating sharks find their prey using their senses of smell and movement and, since sharks have poor eyesight, they may sometimes mistake swimmers and small boats for their usual victims and attack them.

A shark's mouth may be filled with up to 3,000 teeth arranged in many rows. When teeth break or fall out, the shark grows new teeth to replace them.

Most whales eat small sea creatures like fish, squid and plankton. Killer whales (or Orcas) prefer seals, sea-lions, dolphins and walruses. They have been known to attack humans, but this is usually a case of mistaken identity – a human in a black wetsuit looks very like a seal!

Whales, unlike sharks, are mammals, not fish, and have to rise to the surface of the water to breathe as they have no gills. Killer whales can stay under water for up to 20 minutes. They hunt alone or in groups called pods, chasing their prey with great speed. Deep in the oceans there is little light and it is difficult to see, so the whales use sonar, a type of sound wave, to find their victim deep below the water's surface. Killer whales will also grab prey from land and ice, using their strong tails to lift their mouths out of the water.

Birds of Prey

Dagger-like claws and sharp, pointed beaks are the weapons of the world's birds of prey, a group of birds that includes owls, hawks and eagles. These extraordinary and intelligent creatures have the important ability of being able to hunt while flying.

All birds of prey need good eyesight. Most birds have eyes on the sides of their heads, giving good vision all around them; this is important for seeing predators stalking up from behind. Birds of prey have few predators and so their eyes face forwards; this means they can see their victim clearly and can judge distances well. Some birds of prey, like the owl family, hunt at night and these creatures have large eyes that can see even in very dim light.

Birds that hunt need to be fast flyers and can often be seen circling high in the sky, watching their prey beneath them. Some will be hoping to catch another bird in flight, others will be watching small mammals, like mice and rabbits, on the ground below. Once a bird has decided to attack it swoops down at great speed, giving no warning to the intended victim. Huge claws (talons) grab the animal from behind and swoop it up to the sky. The predator takes it away to eat or to feed its hungry brood of babies.

Ospreys are fish-eating birds found throughout the world. Soaring above rivers, lakes and coasts the osprey dives into the water, sometimes disappearing below the surface, to catch a fish. It then flies to a tree or its nest to eat in safety.

25

Crocodiles and Alligators

Walking along the banks of the River Nile in Africa it would be easy to miss the deadly crocodile lurking right next to you. No movement, no noise, not even a twitch of a muscle gives away this large reptile's presence. Just two eyes and two nostrils are poised above the water's still surface searching and sniffing for any passers-by.

Crocodiles are lazy predators; they wait until their supper comes to them, relying on their excellent sense of sight and smell. When an antelope walks to the riverside to drink, this ferocious beast leaps into action. Seizing the antelope with its massive jaws the crocodile swiftly pulls it down into the water, thrashing from side to side until the victim is drowned. A huge mouth, armed with 66 razor-sharp teeth, quickly shreds the flesh from its bones.

Crocodiles and alligators are very similar; they both live in the warm waters of rivers, lakes and coasts. Ruthless meat-eaters, they can kill prey as large as buffalo and wildebeest, although they usually live on fish and smaller mammals. To tell the difference between these two reptiles you need to look at their teeth when their mouths are closed: all of an alligator's bottom teeth are hidden, but two of a crocodile's bottom teeth rest on its upper jaw.

Although deadly to man, crocodiles still play an important part in a river's ecology. Sadly, for many years these creatures were hunted for their skins, which were used to make handbags, belts and shoes. As a result, they became close to being an endangered species. Today this practice has been disallowed.

Snakes

Many people are frightened of snakes and perhaps with good reason. Although few types of snake are dangerous to humans, 30-40,000 people still die each year from snake bites; half of these casualties happen in India.

Snakes usually only kill to eat and will only attack people if threatened. Their favourite prey are small creatures such as mice, frogs and insects.

The king cobra is one of the world's deadliest creatures. When the cobra is attacked it raises its head, like a swan, and sways from side to side. Then it dives forward and sinks its fangs into its victim – pumping poison that can kill a human in eight hours.

The spitting cobra does not use fangs; instead it can spray venom in to its victim's eyes causing great pain and sometimes blindness. The snake then slithers safely away.

Constrictors are the largest snakes, sometimes reaching 13 metres in length. These snakes – the pythons, anacondas and boas – do not use venom to kill their prey. With strong jaws a python bites its victim, such as a gazelle, and wraps itself around the body. When the gazelle breathes out, the snake's coils tighten. With every breath the snake winds itself tighter until the victim can no longer breathe and dies.

As snakes do not have chewing teeth the python must now swallow its meal whole. This may take hours but the snake will not need to feed again for many weeks. Constrictors are shy of humans, but do occasionally attack them.

Fish

Fish have lived on earth for a long time: more than 400 million years. During that time they have adapted to live in all types of watery environment. Now there are thousands of types and sizes of fish living in rivers, lakes, seas and oceans. Many fish graze on aquatic plant-life, but those we might call deadly are either meat-eaters or have developed clever ways to protect themselves.

In the rivers of South America electric eels and shoals of ferocious piranhas swim in search of prey; usually other fish but sometimes larger animals. The electric eel, which grows up to 3 m long, has muscles that can make electricity. It sends electric currents through the water to stun its victims.

Piranhas travel in large groups, or shoals. Smelling by the use of special pits on their noses, they can search out their prey which they rip apart with dagger-like teeth. Even a horse can be quickly reduced to a skeleton this way.

In coastal waters of tropical seas the deadly stonefish lurks. Lying on the sea floor this brown fish has a sharp spine pointing up. A careless bather who steps on it will be injected with a poison which causes terrible pain and is fatal if not treated quickly.

The stingray, another bottom-dweller, causes more injuries to humans than any other fish. By lying flat on the sea floor it remains invisible until disturbed. Then its long tail shoots up and a stinging spine stabs the victim causing pain, weakness and sometimes death.

Spiders and Scorpions

Spiders and scorpions may not look similar but they are close cousins in the animal kingdom; both have eight legs, a hard skin and can kill using deadly venom.

Thankfully, most spiders can kill nothing bigger than an insect. Using webs to catch its prey, the spider sinks its fangs into the flesh and injects the lethal poison.

The female American black widow spider, however, is a ruthless killer. Her venom is strong enough to seriously injure, or even kill, a human but this is unusual. It is the male black widow who is in greatest danger from her because, after mating, the female will try to kill him. She then protects her egg sac until the tiny spiders hatch. When they do, the babies run for their lives – their mother will eat any who are not fast enough.

The bird-eating spider, often known as a tarantula, looks frightening as it is covered with hair and is as large as your hand. However, its bite actually hurts no more than a bee sting does, although the hairs can damage your lungs if breathed in.

Scorpions catch their prey, usually spiders or millipedes, with strong pincers. Their long tails then bend up, over their backs, and the venomous stings are stabbed into the victim.

Scorpions prefer small dark places and it is when they move into houses that they are most likely to harm people. A shoe makes a comfortable nest for the fat-tailed scorpion, whose sting can kill a human within several hours if it is not treated quickly.

Octopus and Jellyfish

Jellyfish do not look like killers as they dance daintily through the water trailing delicate tentacles behind them. But their beauty hides a deadly secret: the tentacles are covered with stinging cells containing venom powerful enough to paralyse fish swimming through them.

The box jellyfish lives in the oceans around Australia and is considered the most dangerous of all jellyfish. Its venom is so powerful it can kill – even humans – extremely quickly. The Portuguese man o' war is similar to a jellyfish but it is really a colony of animals. A gas-filled sac floats on the water's surface while long tentacles hang below. Each tentacle contains many small animals, each with a stinging cell containing poison that kills prey and causes pain and headaches in humans.

Like jellyfish the graceful octopus lives only in salt water and also kills its prey with venom. Gliding silently towards an unsuspecting lobster the octopus slips its tentacles and body over the victim and clings on with its many suckers. A horny beak on the octopus's underside bites the lobster and venom is spat into the wound.

The largest octopus is the Pacific octopus: it grows up to 9 metres in length. The most dangerous is the blue-ringed octopus, found in Australian waters. Although very small, measuring only 20 cm, it contains venom which can kill a human within minutes. Thankfully, octopus and jellyfish prey only on fish and small sea creatures such as crabs and shellfish but any unfortunate humans who come across them may be badly hurt.

Insects - Mini Beasts

Insects are six-legged creatures with a hard outer skeleton (known as an 'exoskeleton'). They are an extremely successful group of animals and can be found in all regions of the world. One of the reasons for the insect group's success is their ability to live anywhere, anyhow.

The ichneumen wasp is a good example of this ability. The female has a long, slender tail that she uses to drill a hole through wood to reach a living sawfly grub. She then lays her eggs on this grub and when the eggs hatch the larvae that emerge eat it alive.

Wasps and bees are famous for their stings which are lethal enough to kill other insects but rarely do more than hurt a human. A honeybee can only sting once: as it flies away part of its body is left attached to the sting, meaning that it will shortly die. However, the sting continues to pump venom into the wound for some time and can produce severe pain.

Bees are kept by farmers to produce honey. Forty years ago two different types of bee were mated in an experiment to try and create a new bee that could make more honey. Unfortunately, the killer bee was created instead. Swarms of these bees have attacked and killed people.

Ants have strong biting jaws and, when they have wounded a victim, are able to squirt into it a chemical, called formic acid, from their tails. African driver ants live in large colonies – swarms of these ants can pass through an area eating every living creature in their path.

Micro Beasts – Blood Suckers and Parasites

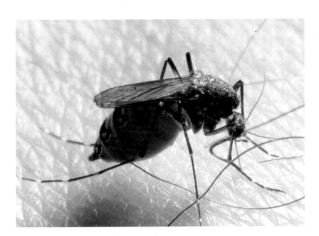

Now we can look at the most deadly group of creatures on this planet: the micro beasts. Too small to be seen, except with a microscope, these animals (micro organisms) are responsible for millions of human deaths every year.

Blood-sucking flies, like the mosquito and the horse fly, enjoy a tasty meal of fresh blood sucked out of an animal or human limb. They may take enough blood to cause illness but the real danger comes from tiny beasts which live in the fly's spit. When a mosquito sucks blood a micro organism, called plasmodium, is injected into a human victim. Plasmodium carries a dreadful disease called malaria that causes illness and death in people all over the world. Mosquitoes also spread yellow fever and dengue fever. Horse flies spread anthrax, and tsetse flies spread sleeping sickness.

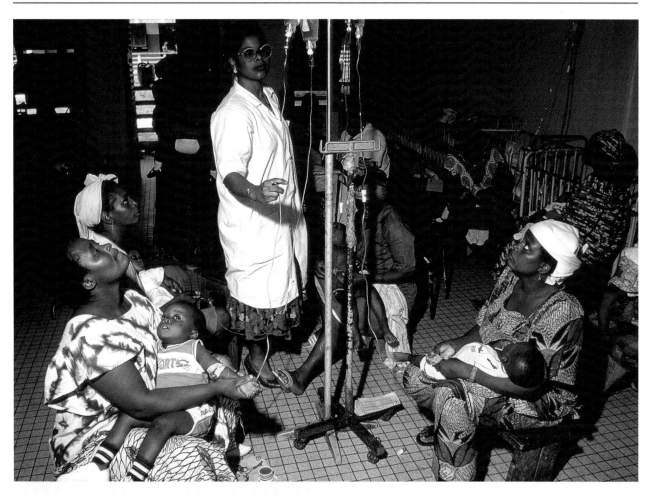

Parasites are creatures that depend on another animal (the host) to live. Fleas are parasites: they need a host to live on and they need to be able to suck its blood. The rabbit flea carries a disease called myxomatosis that is deadly to its host (the rabbit).

The rat flea, though, carries a much more dangerous micro organism: yersinia. This tiny creature is responsible for a terrible illness called plague. Fleas jump between rats, spreading plague – hundreds of millions of people have died from this disease over the centuries. Thankfully, it is much rarer today than in previous centuries because people are better able to keep their homes clean of the dirt which attracts rats.

Defence

Deadly creatures survive by being good at hunting, killing or fighting. Other creatures survive by not getting caught! They do this in many different, clever ways.

One of the best ways to defend yourself is to become invisible. The herds of antelope that graze on the sunburnt plains of Africa are coloured like the grass there, lighter on top and darker below. This shading is also used by fish because it disguises the shape of the animal. The use of colour and shape to hide oneself is called camouflage.

Grazing animals need to stand for a long time while feeding and could be easy prey. They are equipped with a good sense of smell and eyes on the sides of their heads so they can see all around them. These animals usually stand in large groups – there is safety in numbers.

Some animals cleverly mimic others who have a weapon system. The deadly coral snake has bright bands of red, yellow and black. The milk snake does not have poisonous venom but it looks almost the same as the coral snake and any predator will think twice before attacking it.

When frogs are attacked they puff themselves up with air, hoping to make themselves more difficult to swallow. Octopuses and squid shoot clouds of ink-like fluid at any attacker, obscuring the predator's view and giving the intended prey time to turn and swim away.

A lizard caught by his tail can still run away – leaving his tail behind him; in a little while he will grow a new one.

The Balance of Nature

Creatures who are able to hurt and kill others may seem cruel but they have an important role to play in keeping nature balanced. If there were no predators the prey animals would produce more and more young. They would eventually eat all the food and then begin to die themselves.

When lions kill the weakest or ill gazelles they leave the stronger gazelles to breed, producing fitter and stronger calves. When a lion dies, its body helps to fertilise the grasslands that the gazelles can then feed on.

This balance in nature has developed over millions and millions of years. We have our place in nature; we prey upon other animals and are preyed on too. It is also within our power to affect greatly other creatures' lives. Humans destroy the tropical rainforests that are home to many animals and plants; we spray our crops with insecticides that eventually reach the rivers and kill the wildlife in them; we flatten natural habitats to plant trees for wood and paper and we pollute our world and cause global warming.

We can also do things to help. Zoos and wildlife parks look after animals whose homes are being destroyed, they find new ways of helping animals, such as pandas and rare birds of prey, to breed. New ways of controlling pests and parasites are used, ways that do not need chemicals. People can be the deadliest of all creatures, but we can also do a lot to show that we respect the balance of the world's wildlife.

Further Information

Places to Visit

Chester Zoo, Upton, Chester, Cheshire CH2 1LH. Telephone: 01244 380280.

Dartmoor Wildlife Park, Sparkwell, Plymouth PL7 5DG. Telephone: 01752 837209.

Edinburgh Zoo, 134 Corstorphine Road, Edinburgh EH12 6TS. Telephone: 0131 334 9171.

Isle of Wight Zoo, Yaverland, Sandown, Isle of Wight PO36 8QB. Telephone: 01983 403883.

Jersey Zoo, Jersey Wildlife Preservation Trust, Les Augres Manor, Trinity, Jersey JE3 5BP. Telephone: 01534 864666.

London Zoo, Regents Park, London NW1 4RY. Telephone: 0171 722 3333.

Marwell Zoological Park, Colden Common, Winchester SO21 1JH. Telephone: 01962 777407.

The World Owl Trust, Muncaster Owl Centre, Muncaster Castle, Ravenglass, Cumbria CA18 1RQ. Telephone: 01229 717393.

Natural History Museum, Cromwell Road, London SW7 5BD. Telephone: 0171 938 9123.

Welsh Wildlife Centre, Cilgerran, Cardigan SA43 2TB. Telephone: 01239 621600.

Further Reading

The Big Bug Search by Caroline Young, Usborne.
Poisonous Animals by Theresa Greenaway, Dorling Kindersley.
Disguises and Surprises by Claire Llewellyn, Walker.
My Best Book of Creepy Crawlies by Claire Llewellyn, Kingfisher.
Polar Wildlife by Kamini Khanduri, Usborne.
Eyewitness Juniors: Spiders & Poisonous Animals, Dorling Kindersley.
How Green Are You? by David Bellamy, Frances Lincoln.
Wings, Stings and Wriggly Things by Martin Jenkins, Walker.
Grassland Wildlife by Kamini Khanduri, Usborne.
Eyewitness Guide: Shark, Dorling Kindersley.

Picture Credits